Your Free Gift

I wanted to express my appreciation that you support my work so I've put together a free gift for you

31 Healthy Smoothie recipes for month

Just visit the link above to download it now

I'm sure you will love it

Thanks

Chapter One – Dealing With Anxiety

In his book *Believe In Yourself*, Rex Gamble describes anxiety as a thin line of fear running through our veins. I agree completely. I have lived that way most of my life. That thin line of fear affects our attitudes, our moods, our performance, our sleep, our health – well, everything.

It becomes even more serious when it becomes our "normal" way of being and of feeling. Most of the time, we aren't even aware that it's happening. For me, it took an anxiety attack, or a "panic attack", to force me to take a good, honest look under the hood.

If you have never had an anxiety attack, I will try to describe it to you. It's disorientation, kind of a passing out feeling, combined with a cold sweat and loss of feeling in the extremities. Breathing becomes labored and painful, to the point where air is in dangerously short supply. I imagine it's exactly what a heart attack feels like, without the strange comfort of knowing that you might die. Does that sound a little extreme? Well, any of you who have experienced an anxiety attack will agree that it's pretty accurate.

For me, this sequence of events started with that thin line of fear constantly running through my veins. I was perpetually scared of losing what I had and scared of not getting what I wanted. I was always afraid, but with nothing real or tangible to be afraid of. I was terrified of things that were imagined and distorted in my mind, things that only existed between my ears.

It has been shown that ninety percent of what we worry about never happens. Let that sink in for a minute. If that's true, and I believe it is, why do we worry? What do we get out of it? Why can't we just let it go?

I think that we all work very hard and for a very long time to "get on top of things", to control our lives. I want people to drive the right way, I want the people at work to do their jobs the right way, I want my kids to do their chores and education the right way. I want our politicians to govern the right way, I want my favorite team to play the right way. It sounds silly, but think about it. I spend an incredible amount of time and energy worrying about these things. And, of course, the "right way" is the way that *I* would do it. There may be nothing wrong with how they are doing it, but if they aren't doing it the way that I would, it makes me crazy and anxious. And, God forbid something unexpected happens that I didn't plan for. Imagine the chaos that would ensue then.

One very hard truth I've learned about trying to control my life is that life just does what it wants to, despite my objections. I may temporarily have the illusion of control, I may force things into my little box for a minute, but it never lasts very long. Life is messy, and it embarrasses me to think of the time and energy I spend trying to make it neat and orderly. It's like trying to "rope the wind", as Chris LeDoux so eloquently put it.

So, at some point, we have to admit defeat. We have to realize that we have no control whatsoever over other people, or places, or things. Trying to bend life to my will is fruitless and exhausting. Does that mean that I can just quit my job, stop paying my bills and hang around letting life have its way with me? Nope. Because the one thing in life that I *can* control is *me*.

"He can who thinks he can." Orison Swett Marden is credited with that profound statement. Henry Ford put it this way: "Think you can or think you can't. Either way, you're absolutely right."

The human mind is a powerful and amazing thing. Depending on how we use that power, we can choose to achieve great things, or we can choose to defeat ourselves at every turn. In James Allen's book *As A Man Thinketh*, he characterizes the power of the mind this way: "As the plant springs from – and could not be without – the seed, so every act of a man comes from the hidden seeds of thought." So, that means that if I think negative thoughts, I will get negative results. But, of course, if I think positive thoughts, I am sure to get positive results. The law of attraction -like attracts like - is both the problem and the solution. After many years of feeling as though I were at the mercy of life, and everyone and everything in it, I now understand that what I think about most will eventually come about. In my intellectual mind, I know that this is true, and I really do believe it can be that simple.

But, alas, we are not simple creatures. I don't know about you, but I can complicate just about anything. When I think negative thoughts and get negative results, I rationalize and justify and place blame to make myself feel better. And, when I think positive thoughts and achieve positive results, they're usually not exactly the results I wanted, so I tend to dismiss them as not being good enough. In other words, we aren't sure what we want, so it's impossible to focus our energy and our thoughts in a positive direction. If I don't know what I want, chances are good that I'm not going to get it.

I believe that we have choices in every situation, and I can choose to be content or I can choose to be miserable. I can choose to be a victim, or I can choose to take responsibility for my life and my actions. I can choose to do what's in front of me to do, or I can choose to put it off until later, ensuring that I will feel the old anxiety running through my veins again. My friend Rex asks in *Believe In Yourself*, "When do I get that paper written or get the closet cleaned out – when I think about it, when I talk about it, or when I start?" If all I do is worry about something I have to do, or wait for a better time, it can take me much longer than it needs to. On the other hand, if I just start, it's amazing how quickly I get things done and off my mind. Rex also says, "You don't have to be good to start, but you do have to start to be good." I like that a lot.

So, now that I know that my anxiety is caused by worrying about things that I can't control, things that probably won't happen anyway, the next step is to stop worrying. Easier said than done, right? Well, maybe it's not easy, but it is pretty simple. In order to stop worrying about what I don't want, I have to replace that time and energy with something constructive, like deciding what I *do* want. The thing I have to remember though, is that my mind doesn't compute a negative action. For example, if I say "I'm not going to drink anymore" my mind hears "drink" and "more". So, I have to *choose* a positive action to *replace* the action I want to eliminate, and that way I don't trick myself into making things worse. So, my list would look something like this:

To stay focused on the positive things I can do:

1. I choose to do the next right thing.
2. I choose to let go of what I can't control.
3. I choose to accept people, places, things and situations as they are.
4. Once I have identified the problem, I choose to focus my energy and attention on the solution.

5. I choose to put myself in the other person's shoes, so that I can understand where they are coming from.
6. I choose to say "that's interesting", rather than "that's right" or "that's wrong".
7. I choose to be supportive and understanding – chances are that I have made the same mistakes, or will in the future.
8. It's not hard and it's not easy – it just has to be done. So, I choose to do it.
9. I choose to make time for the important things and people in my life. Money is only a means to an end.
10. I choose to remember that everything is not always about me.
11. I choose to stand up for myself. I belong here.

Now it's your turn. Grab a pen and a sheet of paper and write down your "I Choose" list, or your "Action Plan" or whatever you decide to call it, as long as it helps you focus on the things that you can do, right now, to replace anxiety with action.

Chapter Three - Setting and Achieving Goals

What do I want to be? What do I want to do? What do I want to have?

Over the years, I've made many lists, in an attempt to answer each of these questions, hoping desperately that the sky would open up and bless me with the items I wrote down on those pieces of paper. As it turns out, I had the right idea in making the lists. I believe that when I write something down, I'm now responsible for it. And, after I've written it all down, I sign it. Then it becomes a contract. However, my overall goal setting strategy had some fatal flaws.

First, it usually isn't as simple as asking for something and having the Fed Ex guy drop it off that afternoon. I don't just pick up my goals like a pack of tortillas. There is work involved, and I'm the only one who can do it. I have to make a plan and then work toward my goal. It is a conscious, methodical process, not an event. I must be willing to put in the time and effort necessary.

Second, the goal must be *my* goal, not someone else's goal for me. I can't stress this point enough. Well-meaning friends and family members seem to always have ideas about what you can do to be more successful. Countless times in my life, someone has told me, "You should be in sales. With your personality, you can't miss!" And, since other people were in charge of my life, I went into sales a few times. When I tell you I crashed and burned, I want you to picture one of those explosions in a war video game. What I wasn't aware of at the time was that my "personality" was never real. I was always just acting the way that I was expected to act in a given situation. The other thing that became painfully obvious was that I do not have it in me to convince people to do something they don't want to do. Not a glowing trait for a salesman. But I wanted to please people so badly. I would have tried anything to win their approval. If my mother, who I love and admire more than anyone in the world, had told me that I should become a doctor, I would have tried to become a doctor, simply because she suggested it. I would have given it everything I had. But even if, by some miracle, I would have accomplished her goal, I would have been miserable, because it wouldn't have been my goal. On the other hand, if I had an aptitude for it and found that I had a passion for being a doctor, it would have worked out beautifully, because it would have been my goal also. Every goal that I have ever set, until recently, was one that I allowed another person to lay on me. Needless to say, I failed at every single one. When I was a young boy, my dad wanted me to be a professional athlete, and, God how I tried. For years, it was the only thing that mattered to me. I played sports all year, never taking a break from it. And after all that time and effort, after high school, I finally had to admit that I was good, but I wasn't great. I quit, mostly because it was getting in the way of my drinking. The guilt that I carried for having failed my father has hung on me like a lead blanket for decades. The moral of that depressing story is this: set your own goals. Don't allow anyone else to set them for you.

Let's talk about setting our own goals. How do you make sure that your goals are yours and not someone else's? How do you focus on what you really want? First, you should decide what is it that's important to you. Is it money? Health? Freedom? Security? Love? Being part of something larger and greater than you? Helping people? What is it that makes you feel alive? The answer to this question should shape every single goal you write down. But sadly, it doesn't always work that way.

The first time I tried to set goals, I failed. My goals (other people's goals for me) didn't happen. So, I reasoned, the way to not fail at goal setting was to simply not set goals. However, if you want to improve yourself and your life, I don't suggest that method. Knowing what we want and forming a plan to achieve it is crucial if we are going to get where we want to go in this life. For me, however, even to this day, goal setting is hard. It's difficult for me to decide what I want to be, do and have when I have spent my life allowing other people to decide those things for me. The good news is that it gets easier the more I do it.

I grew up thinking that having and making a lot of money was the definition of success. I wanted to be "rich and famous." I did some crazy things, always holding onto the hope that I'd do one great thing, make that big score, and I'd be set for the rest of my life. I wanted to believe that someone would see the obvious greatness in me and see to it that all my dreams came true. I tried out for the Denver Broncos, which didn't go very well. I tried to be an actor, but I didn't like the idea of starting at the bottom. I learned to play guitar and started writing songs, which I actually enjoyed, and still do. I then "took my songs and dreams to Nashville" as Randy Owen sang, and got those doors slammed in my face. I didn't have what it took to accept the failure and rejection and keep striving to achieve my goal. But, no matter how much I failed, I always had it in the back of my mind that I would someday be "discovered", and I would, indeed, be rich and famous. In other words, I was waiting for someone to do it all for me. Not surprisingly, it hasn't happened yet. But I guess it ain't over 'til it's over, right?

There are a few reasons that I failed at becoming rich and famous. Mainly, it's because money is not very high on my list of values. So, when I set a goal to make, let's say, a million dollars this year, all I'm doing is setting myself up to fail. It probably won't happen. As for being famous, my incredibly low self-esteem would never have allowed me to accept the admiration and attention. I would surely have rejected it. So, when I look at my list of goals that I committed to, I feel horrible about myself because I failed. And I know that I will never have a life exceeds my level of self-worth. Therefore, setting myself up for failure just guarantees more failure, because my self-worth just dropped a few notches on the scale. It's an ugly cycle.

So, now I align my goals with my beliefs. How do I do that? Once I have written down a possible goal, I think the goal all the way through and imagine what life would be like once I achieved it. Then, I pay attention to my gut feeling. Most of us don't have much experience trusting what our bodies are trying to tell us, but if you try it, you'll be glad you did. I'll give you an example of how this works for me: Goal: I want to buy a mansion on the beach in Fort Lauderdale. I close my eyes and I think about living in a mansion on the beach in Fort Lauderdale. I see and hear the waves crashing on the shore. I feel the warm breeze on my skin. Then, because I'm me, I think about how astronomical the property taxes would be on a place like that. I think about walking into the house and having to search for forty-five minutes to find my wife. I think about what it would take to clean and maintain the place. I realize that there would probably be at least ten rooms that I would never even see, no matter how long I lived there. Then I remind myself that I have to look at both the positives and the negatives, so, trying to be positive, I tell myself that I could have big parties there, and invite celebrities and politicians and all my friends, and it would be incredible. The problem with that line of thinking is that I hate crowds, and I'm not all that comfortable around people I don't know. I think that trying to impress people is a ridiculous waste of time and energy. If I have a party, I want people around me that I like, people that I choose to be around. The bottom line is that if I pretend that I want a mansion on the beach, I am lying to myself. I can't see myself there. I can't imagine myself enjoying it. It might be what my wife *wants me to want* or what my mother *wants me to want*, or what my kids *want me to want*, but it's not what *I* want. Therefore, it doesn't make the list.

But... let's say I set a goal to buy a nice little house in the neighborhood where I live now. I've always rented – never owned a house. I close my eyes and I imagine myself signing the paperwork and shaking the realtor's hand and smiling. I imagine painting the living room whatever color we want it to be and hanging pictures without worrying about the holes in the walls. I imagine sitting outside with a few friends, fire blazing, talking and singing and roasting marshmallows. I imagine remodeling the kitchen, putting a pool in the back yard, and having our friends over for a swim. That makes me feel warm and happy in my gut. That's a goal that I can get my heart and mind behind. So, it goes on the list, and I'm happy to write it down and sign it, because I can see myself there, and I like the way it feels.

Do you see the difference?

It all comes down to what you want, what you *really* want. For me, that involves getting rid of all of the *should's* and *ought-to's* (you ought to be a salesman, real-estate broker, exotic dancer, etc.) that have had me chasing my tail and running blind in the wrong direction for years. How do I get rid of the *should's* and *ought-to's*? How do I differentiate between the values that are mine and the ones that are somebody else's? The answer to that question, for me, is simple, but not easy. It takes time and effort and absolute self-honesty.

First, let me ask you: What would you do if you suddenly inherited ten million dollars? Think about that for a minute, maybe even make a list (I love lists). Would you buy a house? Quit your job and travel around the world? Walk into the dealership and show that salesman who's boss and walk away with that Range Rover you've always wanted? Buy a brand new wardrobe? The list could go on and on and on. But do you know what is *not* on most people's list? Investing the money wisely and living off the interest. In other words, it's not the money that motivates me. It's the freedom and options that the money provides. So, if I tell myself that my number one goal is having a bunch of money, I will most likely fail, because my goal is not aligned with my beliefs.

So, we're back to the question: What do I want to be, do, and have in this life? To help you answer that question for yourself, I've listed the top five things that people work for. If you'll notice, money is last. Take a minute and honestly think about where they fall in your belief system. Remember, this takes a lot of self-honesty.

1. Recognition
2. A need to belong
3. Security
4. Freedom
5. Money

With your answers to these questions in mind, I encourage you to write down your goals. Don't over-think it, just let yourself dream. Write down what you want to be. Write down what you want to do. Write down what you want to have. Take your time. Let yourself imagine. Watch yourself in your mind's eye doing these things, being in these places. Don't qualify or reason, just dream and see what you get.

Something I learned to do when I finish writing down my goals is to put my papers down and walk away for an hour, or even a day or two, and then come back. I've found that when I separate myself for a while and then come back and look at my goals, I'm able to clarify the ones that work for me and eliminate the ones that don't. And, it usually sparks more ideas.

Once you have written down your goals, and given the process a cooling-off period, it's time to go back and read each goal, paying special attention to how you *feel* while you're thinking about it. If your gut tells you "no", if you can't see yourself there in your mind's eye, then that goal might need to be re-thought, redirected or removed altogether. But if your gut says "yes", if you feel longing and excitement and adrenaline, if you can easily picture yourself there having a wonderful time, then that goal is yours. That one goes on your final list. On a brand-new, clean sheet of paper, write it down, making it a goal that you take responsibility for, and then sign it, making it a contract with yourself. Then, put it in a drawer somewhere. When you come across it a year or two down the road, you'll be amazed how much your life has changed. It's powerful stuff, and it works. Try it. What do you have to lose, besides your negativity and anxiety?

Here's another thing I've learned about goal setting. It never ends. There is no finish line. Am I going to just sit alone in the house I've always wanted with my Camaro parked in the driveway, listening to my songs on Pandora? Maybe for a day or two, but then what? I have to come up with some more goals to work toward, right? I can't just stop living. So, I have made getting good at goal setting a goal in itself. After all, the fun is in the journey anyway.

Chapter Four – Positive Thinking

For a long time, I felt guilty about the fact that I didn't think positively as often as I should. The successful people I knew always talked about positive thinking, and there are countless books on the subject, so I knew that I was supposed to think positively. The problem was that I didn't know how, and I was too ashamed to ask, because I was afraid of looking stupid. You see, I always felt like, when they were handing out the instruction manual for life, I was absent that day. I was ashamed and embarrassed that I didn't know everything that everybody else in the word knew. I thought that I should know how to do it all, including thinking positively.

So, I worked very hard at looking like I was being positive. I smiled when I guessed I was supposed to smile, and I tried to sound and look as though I knew what I was doing. I never talked about problems, because "problems are just opportunities in disguise." I attended seminars about positive thinking, and that made me feel even more like an impostor. Whatever the situation, I wanted everyone to think that I had it handled. To be fair to myself, there were some things that I was good at. But when it came to the things that I didn't know or understand, I was afraid to ask anyone to show me or explain them to me. I believed that I was supposed to know it all already, and I couldn't let anybody see that I didn't. The result of all of this was that I never grew as a person. I never learned anything new, because I wouldn't admit that I didn't know.

Now I understand that positive thinking applies to the idea of improvement, not perfection. I know now that, if I can maintain a positive attitude, I can open my mind enough to allow myself to learn something. Then, maybe I can do a little bit better today than I did yesterday. That's growth right there, and I'll take it. But for me to get to a place where I could begin that growth, I had to accept myself exactly where I was. This is where that make-believe positive thinking really got me in trouble. If I was unwilling to admit that I had any faults or weaknesses, if I was always "great", then I gave myself no starting point.

The truth is, I have never achieved or accomplished anything worthwhile without someone's help. Not one time. So, that's proof right there that I don't know everything. I had to have learned something from someone to know what I knew, right? So, once I started getting more honest with myself, and chipped away at the foolish idea that I had to be perfect to be liked and accepted, I was able to see myself more clearly, the way others saw me. I had to learn to keep the self-judgement and fear from creeping in and just look at what was really there. I had to peel away the layers of negative judgements from the world, my peers, and even myself. There was no room for performances, emotions, or excuses. And what I saw, when I really looked for the first time, was, well, not all great and not all bad. I saw a man, just like everybody else. I saw that I could stand to miss a meal or two, but I was doing pretty well for a middle-aged ex-jock. Then it hit me, full-force, that I had come a long way. And acknowledging that growth in myself bumped up my self-worth, which made it that much more likely that I could continue to grow.

Where I have to be careful, with regards to positive thinking, is confusing positive thinking with proper thinking. Positive thinking is crucial and necessary when I need to stay encouraged, tackle a difficult task, and believe in myself. But there are also times when a negative approach is a very effective one. With regard to goal setting, using the example about the mansion on the beach vs. the nice little house, by realizing that the mansion was not one something I wanted or cared about, I was able to eliminate that from my mind, and free up more space in my head to think about things that I *do* want. If I were to use positive thinking in that situation rather than proper thinking, I might still be telling myself that I should want that mansion, because, by golly, I'm a winner! As magnificent as the mind is, I can still confuse it and overload it with ideas that don't need to be there. And, as I get older, I find that I just don't have that much room in my brain anymore, and I'm not able to remember most of what I know. So, by using proper thinking rather than positive thinking, I can keep the thoughts that are working for me, and get rid of the ones that are confusing my mind, and pointing my compass in the wrong direction.

There is not enough time in our lives to learn everything the hard way. Therefore, I am going to share with you some of my favorite quotes about positive thinking, from people who have proven, in their own lives, that it works:

"Think you can, or think you can't... either way, you're absolutely right." – Henry Ford

"You can, you should, and – if you're brave enough to start – you will." – Stephen King

"We can complain because rose bushes have thorns, or we can rejoice because thorn bushes have roses." – Abraham Lincoln

"If it is to be, it is up to me." – Rex Gamble

"I could have missed the pain, but I'd have had to miss the dance." – Garth Brooks

I'm sure you could come up with a great list of your own. In fact, why don't you?

Life can be hard. I know, for most of us, that is an understatement. But sometimes, when I'm feeling especially sorry for myself, I think about some of the people that I admire most, and I become humbled and grateful to be who I am and to have what I have. People like Stevie Wonder, Ronnie

Milsap, Ray Charles and Jeff Healy, just to name a few, who reached great heights and accomplished amazing things, not in spite of, but *because of* the fact that they are blind. My music teacher in elementary school lost a finger in Viet Nam, and when he came home he learned to play piano because it was hard. My wife, Elizabeth, is recovering from breast cancer surgery, and she feels pain that I can't even comprehend all day every day. She still lights up the room and brightens the lives of everyone she touches. People have an incredible capacity for greatness. I just have to remember that I am one of them.

When I see things from that perspective, I realize that the only thing that can stop me from accomplishing anything I want to do in this life is the six inches between my ears. Everything in life is a choice. Choose wisely.

Chapter Five – Relationships

I am blessed to be the father of three sons. They are all grown men now, but my youngest still lives with me. This gives me a wonderful opportunity to share my growth and the things that I learn on a constant basis. Much of what I learn about life comes from his amazing mind and heart, and from the honest, unashamed exchange of ideas between us. It is a wonderful relationship and I'm grateful for it. I never had the same opportunity with my older boys, but correcting that situation is one of my major goals in life.

It is my belief that one of the most pressing issues we have in our country is that we men don't know how to be men. I think it started with my generation, when divorce became socially acceptable and more common, when moms went to work, and boys didn't have their dads around. Sadly, it seems that the problem has grown worse with each new generation.

The days of a father and son working side by side seem to be, largely, a thing of the past. The time we do spend together, in most cases, is spent doing things separately. With so many things to distract us, it seems that people on the other side of the country and the world are more important to us than the people in the next room. Fewer families have meals together. We're all so busy that we don't have time for each other. So, who is teaching our boys to be men? Unfortunately, no one is. A boy needs, and will always need, the guidance of an older man. If not his father, then an uncle or a professor or a coach needs to step up. The problem is that we don't step up; either because we tell ourselves that it's not our problem, or because, having had no one to teach us, what could we possibly pass on to someone else that is of any use?

And even if - as in my case - a father has the good fortune of spending a good deal of quality time with his son, we're still crippled by the fact that many men my age did not have a man there to show us how to be men. My father was a nice guy, and I loved him, but he was a drunk, and all I learned from him was how to drink, hide and give up. With an example like that, how am I supposed to teach my son anything he can use? The only thing I can do is be as good a dad as I can be and teach him what I have learned from a lifetime of doing it the wrong way. If I handle it properly, my failures can be the most important asset I have as a father. I know that's difficult for a lot of you to wrap your minds around – we're supposed to be pillars of strength and righteousness – but we have to use what we have, and my crazy life is all I have to offer. Thankfully, I have had help from some incredible people who taught me how to accept myself and how to be thankful for who I am and what I have. If that's the worst thing I pass on to my kids, it's okay with me. The good news is that honesty is contagious. If I can tell the truth and laugh at myself, it makes it okay for other people to do the same. Sometimes we underestimate the importance of just talking to each other like people.

I believe that just about everything in life comes in degrees. I'm anxious and afraid to a far lesser degree than I used to be, and that's progress that I need to recognize and celebrate. But when I do worry, when something is bothering me, and that thin line of fear is coursing through my veins, I tend to handle it like a guy; I isolate myself from other people, and tell myself that I have to handle things on my own. I always believed that talking to someone about a problem was whining, and the one thing that I could never allow myself to be was a whiner. So, now I have a choice. I can handle my anxiety the way I always have, alone in my suffering, and let it eat me up, or I can do something different. I can choose to ask for help. This is something that men don't do well, but it's amazing how much more efficient and effective it is than the other way. It's the same concept as not asking for directions. It doesn't make any sense to be so stubborn about things, but we still are. I think what holds us back from asking for help, many times, is that it starts with the admission that we don't have the answers. But I will tell you that the second I make that dreaded admission and ask someone to help me, my anxiety level drops to about half. I can almost hear it land. A shared burden is a much lighter one.

As for romantic relationships, I think the same things apply. If I'm honest and admit it when I don't know, and I ask for help when I need it, things go much more smoothly. Unfortunately, though, we tend to approach a romantic relationship differently than other relationships. In my experience, even when I've started to do the right things in the other aspects of my life, when I've started making good decisions and setting proper goals, and changing the things I wanted to change, I revert back to my old, anxiety-ridden, fearful self when it comes to my relationships with women. I approached it like it was either a Disney movie or a knife fight.

Throughout my first two failed marriages, I thought that my job was to be the answer to everything. I expected myself to earn enough money that my wives didn't have to work. I expected myself to handle the bills and make all of the decisions about houses, cars, etc. I expected myself to do whatever it took to create a situation where my wives didn't have to worry about anything. Well, not only did I fail extravagantly at each of these, I missed the point of a relationship entirely. The word "relation", all by itself, suggests and requires at least two people, right? Why in the world did I think I was going to do it all on my own?

But the worst thing that happened was that the message that I sent them was, "I don't need you." I also, unknowingly, sent the message that I didn't think they could handle anything, that they weren't good enough. So, when I inevitably crashed and burned, there was no "relationship" to fall back on. They had long since stopped caring.

Now, I am blessed to be with the most amazing woman in the world, but it took me being alone for many years to finally wrap my head around relationships and my role in them. One of the main things that I must remember and live by is that I have no control over people, places and things. This includes my wife. I've always operated under the mistaken idea that the rules were different in a marriage. No, they're not. She is another person – a person all on her own, with or without me. And, by rule, that means that I have no control over her.

This is where trust comes in. Until I finally got tired of myself and made some changes, I was excruciatingly jealous and insecure. If you have ever been in a relationship with a jealous person, you know just how awful it is. You do everything you can do not to arouse suspicion or cause problems, but it doesn't help. A truly jealous person will see things that aren't there. When you are dealing with a person like this, you have two choices: shut down completely, or break free and do what you want to do, pretty much guaranteeing the end of the relationship. I would guess that the second option would be the best option in just about every case.

But jealousy, believe it or not, tears the offender apart as well. It's horrible to know that you have no reason to think the things you're thinking, but not be able to stop thinking them. The fear is so powerful that it can't be controlled. It consumes you. And, like a tornado that is borne from a hurricane, the guilt and self-loathing make life all but impossible for everyone involved.

I spent the better part of forty years in and out of relationships and marriages that I destroyed because of my insecurity and jealousy. In the process, I caused some very good people to question themselves, and I regret that fact most of all. The good news, though, is that it doesn't have to be that way. It's not as simple as making the decision that I don't want to be that way anymore, and then expect it all to fix itself, but it is a beginning. I have found that I have an incredibly high tolerance for my own stupidity, but when I finally reach the point where I can't live with myself, I begin to look for answers. And the answers are always, 100% of the time, between my ears. It never is, and never has been, the other person's wrongdoing. It is always inside my head.

So, as I said previously, changing starts with the bitter, naked, bare-bones, nasty truth. I had to accept the ugly fact that I was weak and insecure and afraid, and that it was no one's fault but my own. Next, I had to forgive myself. This took some time, but I find that when I'm dealing with the simple truth, it's not nearly as hard as working from the standpoint of what I *should* think or *should* feel or *should* do. The truth eliminates a bunch of worthless thought and wasted energy.

We have established that to remove something negative from our lives, we have to replace it with something positive, right? Otherwise, we leave a void, and something worse than what we wanted to replace could very well come along and fill it. So, that being true, can we get rid of our anxiety, or at least experience it to a much smaller degree? Of course we can. And I have just the thing to replace it with – serenity. Now, to be honest, if you had asked me five years ago what serenity was, I would not have been able to tell you. But now I know what serenity is, and it has become my mission, for the rest of my life, to choose serenity over anxiety. Because serenity is, in my opinion, the greatest gift on this earth.

We talked about that thin line of fear running through our veins when we are anxious, and I described what an anxiety attack is like. So, with that in mind, let me also point out that this is not a once-in-awhile event. It is my experience that when I'm anxious about one thing, I'm usually anxious about everything. I have a hard time sleeping, or I sleep too much. I always feel lethargic, exhausted and depressed. It's awful. Even more so when it has become my normal state. When I feel this way, rather than facing my problems, I hide from them, which causes even more anxiety. This added anxiety from not dealing with my life causes my problems get larger and multiply. There is never any peace, never any rest. I am irritable and unhappy and very difficult to be around.

On the other hand, when I am serene, I'm at ease in any situation. I like people, and I make time for the ones I love and want to spend my time with. I don't worry about what people think of me, because it's none of my business. My best is always good enough, take it or leave it. It's easy for me to admit when I'm wrong and apologize. Problems don't cripple me, they bring out the best in me. I don't try to be better than anyone else, because I understand that I am just as good as anyone on this planet – not better or worse, but just as good – and I belong here, just like you do. I have earned my place at the table. I laugh more. I don't try nearly as hard and I get more done. People want to be around me, because they know exactly what they are going to get from me. They can rest. The chaos that has always been the driving force of my life has been replaced by calm. I have no expectations of other people, therefore, I am always pleasantly surprised.

As you're reading this, you're probably wondering how an old, washed up drunk who has failed his entire life, could possibly know anything about serenity, and I don't blame you. I can assure you it's nothing that I did. Most of the work involved in bringing me from anxiety to serenity was just letting go of the people, activities, ideas and beliefs that weren't working in my life. It's truly that simple.

I guess that, for me, the catch was that I had to reach a jumping-off point before I was able to make some positive choices. Let's face it, if what I had been doing was giving me what I wanted, no matter how harmful, I wouldn't have had a reason to change, right? It would have been easy to go on lying and cheating and stealing and drinking, if there had never been any consequences. Thankfully, though, life has a way of knocking us on our butts and forcing us to take a look at ourselves. I just hope it doesn't wait as long with you as it did me.

My jumping-off point was probably what you would expect. I was homeless, penniless, friendless, jobless, and I had managed to burn every bridge I had ever walked across. No one would help me anymore. People had had enough of me – bartenders, friends, family, employers, everyone. There were no more chances. I wanted to kill myself, but didn't have the courage. I couldn't go on one more minute the way that I had been. This painful, desperate state of affairs has proven to be the greatest gift I ever received, because it finally got my attention, and forced me to take some positive action. I found people who were willing to help me, and they showed me that it didn't have to be the way it was. Since then, it has been quite a journey, and along the way, I found serenity. And through this process, I have learned that the little things that once threw me into a tailspin don't matter. I don't worry about what people are going to say or do. I don't allow people to dictate what I should say or do. I no longer give people the power to hurt me. I am always honest, because it's exhausting trying to keep track of the lies. I no longer place my expectations on the shoulders of the people I care about. It's a great way to live, and I recommend it. The cool thing about it is that you don't have to be suicidal, or be a drunk or addict to achieve serenity. It's right there for all of us. We just have to make a little room.

Unfortunately, achieving serenity, at least in my experience, is not like turning a switch on and off. At the same time, it's not as hard as you might think, either. For me, it was simply a matter of deciding I wasn't going to fight life any more. I realized that, the harder I fought against it, the worse it got. I never won. Never. It's like pushing *out* as hard as you can on a door that opens *in*. It just closes tighter and tighter. And, since I can't remove a negative without leaving a void, I replace fighting with faith. The kind of faith I'm talking about is not necessarily religion, but it does involve the realization that my way isn't working, so I need to do something different. It's admitting that, the harder I try to control life, the less control I actually have.

When most of us think about letting go of the control of our lives, it's horrifying. Changing anything that we've been doing our whole lives is always frightening. And it takes some time. We have to remind ourselves repeatedly to let go. We have to talk to ourselves, remind ourselves that we don't have any control over that person or that situation. It must become a habit, and that will take whatever time it takes. I can't throw a lemon seed out in the back yard and expect to have a lemon tree the next morning. What I'm saying is that it's different than most of our goals and aspirations, because the point is doing less rather than doing more.

What I discovered when I began this process a few years ago, was that things just have a way of working themselves out, whether I worry about them or not. Another happy result was that I suddenly had time to do things to improve myself and my life. When I focused on working on myself rather than trying to fix everybody else, my life improved quickly. And, ironically, I found that I was, indeed, in charge of things. I now have absolute control over my own thoughts and actions. I am no longer reacting to people and circumstances. I now live on purpose.

Going back to James Allen's little book, *As A Man Thinketh*, he puts it this way: "A person is buffeted by outside circumstances as long as he believes himself to be at the mercy of outside conditions." The first time I read this book was in 1982, when I was eighteen years old, and with my undeveloped and twisted belief system, I thought he meant that I had to take control of everything. I thought it meant that I had to force myself upon the world and take what I wanted. Thankfully I knew, even then, that I didn't have that in me.

But now, after many years of trial and error, I have gained a little bit of wisdom. And I understand that I have lived my entire life like a hockey goalie. I had shots flying at me relentlessly, from everywhere, and I felt like the entire world was out to beat me. I hoped that I could have enough control to stop a shot here and there, but I knew in my heart that there was no way I was going to win. The worst part of it all was that quitting and walking away from it didn't seem like an option. It felt like there was no way out. So, every day, knowing that I was going to lose, embarrassed and ashamed about that fact but not able to change it, I went back out there and got knocked around.

Now I know that I don't have to be the goalie. I don't have to be the victim f I don't want to. I am the leading man – the hero – in my story. Nobody else can be. It's my story, no one else's. And how I write that story, what I do with that power – is completely up to me. Don't get me wrong – I still have to deal with other people and outside forces. The difference is that I no longer have to be at their mercy. I no longer have to give them power over me. I can choose to walk away from people and situations that are unhealthy for me. I don't need the approval of the entire world any more. I am in charge of my life. I belong here.

Chapter Seven – Relaxation and Meditation

Our world doesn't lend itself easily to the idea of doing nothing. It seems that we're always running, always striving, scrambling to gain control of our world. And now, in the age of social media and instant information and gratification, we're afraid to step away, because we might miss something. But I believe that we absolutely must take time for ourselves. We have to create a place where it's just us, alone with our thoughts. It is vital to our serenity.

Finding a place for our mind to unburden itself, and the time to allow for it, can be a challenge for most of us. For some, it may be going to the gym and running on the treadmill, for others it may be going to the park. Many people think their best very early in the morning, when the rest of the world is still sleeping. For my wife, it's a bubble bath with candles and smooth jazz in her earbuds. Whatever it takes, we must find that time and space.

I have a little corner in the Florida room of our house that belongs to me. For you northerners, a Florida room is a room at the back of the house that looks out into the back yard. In many cases, it is kind of separated from the rest of the house. Some Florida rooms are screened in, some have a pool in them, etc. However it's set up, the point of a Florida room is to leave the worries and tribulations of the day back behind us, in the main part of the house. It's supposed to be a sanctuary or a refuge where we can get away from life for a little while. Ours in fully enclosed, but it has a beautiful view of the trees in our yard, and it can be a quiet place under the right circumstances. We also use it as a music room/recording room, dining room, and meeting place. In my little corner, I have my desk, my computer, my guitar, and a couple of awards and diplomas. It's a place where I can look at what is right about me, what is right with the world, and what is good and special in my life. Everybody in the house knows that this is my corner, and when I disappear to my corner, I'm usually working. So, many times, this is a good place for me to be alone. Sometimes, though, being alone is just not in the cards. There are times that I go and hang out in the garage or go for a drive instead. Other times, I simply outlast the others and take my quiet time after they've gone to bed. But, whatever it takes, I must create that time and space for myself. It is not an option.

Once I am in my quiet place, the first thing I have to do is shut off the voices, the noises, the reminders, the alarms in my mind. I have to silence the racing thoughts in my head about my schedule, what I have to do at work, how I'm going to pay the electric bill, and on and on. Doing this takes time and practice, but it's well worth it.

My next thought is always "thank you". This directs my mind to think about what I have and what I'm grateful for, rather than what I don't have. This, more than anything else, allows me to replace anxiety with serenity, to replace chaos with tranquility. The world can be losing its collective mind right outside my door, but for this short time that I am in this space, I know peace. I can breathe. I can put things in perspective, and see what is important and what isn't. I can choose between the worthless and the worthwhile. Now, this is where I need to be careful not to talk about God or Bhudda or Allah or Whoever, for fear of offending someone or leaving someone out. Whatever God may or may not be, God can only be, to me, what I believe God to be. All I know for sure is that there is a Power that is much greater and larger than little old me. In addition, as I've said previously, my way doesn't work, and it never has. But this Higher Power's way seems to work just fine. So, call it what you want to, but I believe there is a voice within me, and that voice is what I reach out to during my alone time. And, any time that I approach anything from the standpoint of gratitude, I know that my mind is in the right place.

Something that was very difficult for me to learn was that these conversations are meant to be just that – a conversation, a dialogue. Too many times, I treat it like it's a monologue, and I'm the only one talking. Sometimes I have to remember to just shut my mouth, silence my mind and give it another minute, take a little more time to listen.

I'm still learning about all of this, and I imagine I will be learning about it until the day I die. I don't think it's anything we ever master, simply because the answers never come to us the same way twice. The answers can come from anywhere – books, songs, road signs, anywhere. The secret, for me, is to be open to them when they come. What is important about my quiet time, meditation, whatever your name for it, is that when I go within to ask questions, I must accept the answers I get. Then, when the time comes for those answers to translate into actions, I'll know I'm headed in the right direction.

I'm still hoping to hear that huge, booming voice from above, but I haven't yet. My wife hears the voice all the time. I guess it's different for all of us. But, for me, the answers are all about hindsight. I'll be going through something I can't handle, and I'll ask for help. I never hear anything right away, because I haven't reached that level of acceptance yet. So, I just forget about it for a while. But, amazingly, when I look back in a couple of weeks or months, I see that it worked out beautifully, without any conscious effort on my part. Trust me, I wouldn't believe it if I wasn't living it.

A wonderful byproduct of approaching my quiet time with gratitude in my heart is that it works hand-in-hand with the power of my mind. If I think about what I'm grateful for, I am programming my mind to bring more of what I want into my life.

There is no one "right way" to meditate. The practice is as old as time, and people have been introducing and perfecting techniques for ages. Like anything else, though, it comes down to finding a technique that works for you. I will touch on some methods and techniques that you can try on for size, and you can mix and match and find the right combination of activities, for you, that will give you the peace, relaxation, and clarity of thought that you seek.

The method that works best for me, which I think of as "focusing", but is also called "concentration", involves focusing on one area of the body at a time. This could be concentrating on your breathing; the sound, the rhythm, the number of breaths in and out, etc. Another method of "focusing" that I use, which I borrowed from author Martha Beck's *Finding Your Own North Star*, is to focus on one body part at a time, starting with each toe, and working your way up to your head. She suggests that you concentrate on how it feels: Is it cold? Does it hurt or ache? Is the nail too long? The idea is to think only of that toe until there is nothing else that you can add, and then do the same with the next body part. I have to confess that I have never made it past my left knee before I fell asleep, but that's a blessing in and of itself. The point is to clear your mind of everything except that single part of the body, which allows you to temporarily release and let go of all of the chaos going on in your life and your mind.

Another method is to relax and allow your thoughts to wander where they will. The idea is to pick one thought and just follow it wherever it leads you. What is crucial to the success of this method is to just allow the thought to be, without judging it as right or wrong, good or bad. I think of it as standing aside and watching my thoughts go by. For me, this method is different than focusing in that, rather than forcing my mind to concentrate on something, I'm allowing it not to concentrate at all.

An exercise that I have learned, involving the power of the mind, is based on the idea that what we think about will come about. This could be used in preparation for an event, such as a presentation or a performance. It requires closing your eyes and seeing yourself, in your mind's eye, performing the action. You envision your clothes, your hair, the other people in the room, the sounds, the smells, the lights. You imagine how you feel; are you nervous, excited? Then, picture your execution of the presentation or performance. Picture it going exactly the way you want it to. If you do this exercise over and over, you will train your mind to do it exactly as you envisioned. This method of meditation is used by athletes, performers, trainers, and it will work for you too. I can tell you, personally, that, while I haven't always had the self-discipline to do this on purpose, there have been times that I have learned an entire song on the guitar, just by seeing the strings and the frets and my fingers in my mind. The human mind is a wonderful and amazing apparatus and, sadly, we use only about ten percent of its power. But we don't have to let it stay that way. We can change how we use the power of our minds any time we choose to.

These methods of mediation, and, I'm sure, countless others, are available to us any time we want them. The important thing about any type of self-reflection is to set the stage – let go of the things that are swimming around in our heads – and find the time and the place to allow ourselves the opportunity to take care of ourselves. To many of us, demanding this time feels selfish, but I believe it is vital to our mental, physical and spiritual health.

Through my experiences, my mistakes, and the fact that I have survived, I have learned to stop fighting. I have learned acceptance. I have learned to let go of people, places and things over which I have no control. I've learned that, to get what I want, I must first *know* what I want – I must be able to see it in my mind, to define it and explain it. I have learned that life's problems, other peoples' problems, most of the things I worry about, are not always about me.

Most importantly, I've learned that I'm just as good as anyone on this planet, and *I belong here.*

So do you.

Your Free Gift

Once again I wanted to express my appreciation that you support my work so I've put together a free gift for you

31 Healthy Smoothie recipes for month

Just visit the link above to download it now

Please share your opinion about this book, review it on Amazon

Thanks a million!

www.ingramcontent.com/pod-product-compliance
Lightning Source LLC
Chambersburg PA
CBHW070243290526
45789CB00004B/1749